◇◇

SACRED
FEMININE
◦RACLE

SACRED FEMININE ORACLE

divine healing

MALORY MALMASSON

ILLUSTRATED BY MARION BLANC

ROCKPOOL

A Rockpool book
PO Box 252
Summer Hill
NSW 2130
Australia

rockpoolpublishing.com

Follow us! f 🄾 rockpoolpublishing
Tag your images with #rockpoolpublishing

Original French edition © 2021, Éditions Contre-Dires,
a Guy Trédaniel publishing house.

This edition published in 2022 by Rockpool Publishing

ISBN: 9781922579416

Edited by Jess Cox
Design by Sara Lindberg, Rockpool Publishing

Printed and bound in China
10 9 8 7 6 5 4 3 2 1

CONTENTS

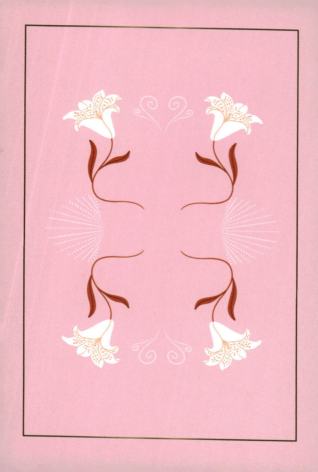

INTRODUCTION

This oracle is a fun tool, providing women with keys, messages and exercises to accompany them on their journey into their sacred femininity. It honours feminine energy, yin, creativity, receptivity and being able to unify, be an alchemist and connect with subtle energies and inner feelings. This oracle invites you to reconnect with your original power, from which you have been dispossessed because of our patriarchal culture.

WHAT IS SACRED FEMININITY?

The sacred feminine is the manifestation of our female principle – its qualities, values and energies. These female principles must be allied with the manifestation of male principles, because although masculine and feminine energies appear to be opposed they are in fact polarities waiting to unite for greater harmony and balance. Each human being possesses these energies to a different degree. By exploring and assimilating them we can reveal qualities left hidden or dormant until now. By revealing these principles the masculine and feminine energies cooperate, mutually uplifting each other. We can then celebrate their inner alchemic marriage, which helps us to recover a feeling of unity, fullness and completeness.

WHAT ARE THE ISSUES OF OUR TIME?

The time has come for men and women to reconnect with their sacred masculine and feminine – with their ancestral power – and release their accumulated wounds. All are invited to rediscover their greatness and ability to enchant the world; meet with themselves deeply, intimately and truly, revealing their true nature; affirm their many qualities and express their beauty to return magic into life and poetry into society; and contribute to there being greater meaning and harmony.

STRUCTURE
OF THE
ORACLE

This oracle includes 43 cards. The first 42 cards are divided into seven colour-coded families; each family contains six cards belonging to one of six categories.

CATEGORIES	ARCHETYPES		
	THE AMAZON	THE MATRIARCH	THE CHILD-WOMAN
RESOURCES AND QUALITIES	1. Independent	7. Loyal	13. Receptive
WOUNDS	2. Threatened	8. Unappreciated	14. Abused
RELATIONSHIPS, LOVE AND SEXUALITY	3. Empowered	9. Committed	15. Indecisive
SHADOWS	4. Untameable	10. Quarrelsome	16. Self-centred
CHAKRAS	5. Grounded	11. Tantric	17. Ferrywoman
SELF-KNOWLEDGE AND EXPRESSION	6. Determined	12. Devoted	18. Guide

THE MATERNAL WOMAN	THE SENSUAL WOMAN	THE ACCOMPLISHED WOMAN	THE MYSTIC WOMAN
19. Loving	25. Alchemic	31. Wise	37. Peaceful
20. Lacking	26. Unrecognised	32. Abandoned	38. Neglected
21. Unconditional	27. Inspiring	33. Reasoned	39. Solitary
22. Invasive	28. Seductive	34. Demanding	40. Wild
23. Healer	29. Expressive	35. Psychic	41. Oracle
24. Generous	30. Creative	36. Warrior	42. Aligned

The final card is the Goddess card, a special card beyond families and categories.

THE SEVEN FAMILIES

The seven families are distinguished by their colours, with each embodying the energy of a feminine archetype.

THE ARCHETYPES

An archetype is a symbolic representation of an energy present in society or an emblematic figure of historical significance. Each archetype carries qualities and values, memories and wounds; it embodies attributes and a mission; and it lives in our collective unconscious.

These archetypes are present in every woman even if some are more pronounced than others. The purpose of these archetypes is to help you shine your full potential, reveal your feminine but also heal wounds, abuse and the domination that women have suffered for so long.

Red cards represent the Amazon, the wild woman in touch with her instincts. This archetype includes the following cards:

THE AMAZON
1. Independent
2. Threatened
3. Empowered
4. Untameable
5. Grounded
6. Determined

Orange cards represent the Matriarch, the keeper of traditions. This archetype includes the following cards:

THE MATRIARCH
7. Loyal
8. Unappreciated
9. Committed
10. Quarrelsome
11. Tantric
12. Devoted

Yellow cards represent the Child-woman. This archetype includes the following cards:

THE CHILD-WOMAN
13. Receptive
14. Abused
15. Indecisive
16. Self-centred
17. Ferrywoman
18. Guide

Green cards represent the Maternal Woman, the nurturing mother. This archetype includes the following cards:

THE MATERNAL WOMAN
19. Loving
20. Lacking
21. Unconditional
22. Invasive
23. Healer
24. Generous

Blue cards represent the Sensual Woman, inspiring and inspired. This archetype includes the following cards:

THE SENSUAL WOMAN
25. Alchemic
26. Unrecognised
27. Inspiring
28. Seductive
29. Expressive
30. Creative

Indigo cards represent the Accomplished Woman, the business woman and counsellor. This archetype includes the following cards:

THE ACCOMPLISHED WOMAN
31. Wise
32. Abandoned
33. Reasoned
34. Demanding
35. Psychic
36. Warrior

Purple cards represent the Mystic Woman. This archetype includes the following cards:

THE MYSTIC WOMAN
37. Peaceful
38. Neglected
39. Solitary
40. Wild
41. Oracle
42. Aligned

A final white card represents the Goddess. She is fully aligned in her sacred feminine, unifying each archetype and expressing them all freely without restraint or fear.

THE GODDESS

THE SIX
CATEGORIES

**THERE ARE SIX CATEGORIES
INCLUDED IN THIS ORACLE:**

Resources and qualities

Wounds

Relationships, love and sexuality

Shadows

Chakras

Self-knowledge and expression

Through these categories, I invite you to:

1. Discover and express your resources and qualities. These cards picture animals surrounded by symmetrical patterns. Each card invites you to recognise or develop these qualities.

RESOURCES AND QUALITIES
1. Independent
7. Loyal
13. Receptive
19. Loving
25. Alchemic
31. Wise
37. Peaceful

2. Treat your wounds by engaging in a process of inner healing. These cards present figures of women. Each card suggests a visualisation and a mantra to console, appease and heal your wounded self.

WOUNDS
2. Threatened
8. Unappreciated
14. Abused
20. Lacking
26. Unrecognised
32. Abandoned
38. Neglected

3. Balance your relationships, but also attain fulfilment in your love and sex lives. These cards depict symbols surrounded by plants and symmetrical patterns. Each card offers advice in matters of love and sexuality.

RELATIONSHIPS, LOVE AND SEXUALITY
3. Empowered
9. Committed
15. Indecisive
21. Unconditional
27. Inspiring
33. Reasoned
39. Solitary

4. Regulate excesses brought on by your shadows. These cards represent female figures surrounded by animals. Each card invites you to question your excesses and adjust them with the help of reminders or wisdom teachings.

SHADOWS
4. Untameable
10. Quarrelsome
16. Self-centred
22. Invasive
28. Seductive
34. Demanding
40. Wild

5. Expand your chakras and discover your alchemical forces. These cards show landscapes. Each card offers counsel and a positive affirmation mantra.

CHAKRAS
5. Grounded
11. Tantric
17. Ferrywoman
23. Healer
29. Expressive
35. Psychic
41. Oracle

6. Know and encounter yourself, fully opening yourself to the world and embodying your full potential. These cards present portraits of women. Each card offers personal growth and spiritual messages aided by challenges, allowing you to discover and express what lies in your innermost depths.

SELF-KNOWLEDGE AND EXPRESSION
6. Determined
12. Devoted
18. Guide
24. Generous
30. Creative
36. Warrior
42. Aligned

CREATING SPREADS

RECOMMENDATIONS

Presented here are a few different spreads, but feel free to develop your own way of reading the cards by following your intuition and letting your inner voice guide you. You can set an intention or think of a question before creating a spread to obtain an answer or advice. If you haven't got a specific request to make don't worry; you can just ask to receive guidance towards your fulfilment or evolution.

To avoid influencing the reading when you shuffle the cards and select one, don't think too much about the kind of response you'd like to receive.

If one or more cards turn over by themselves or slip out of the deck when you shuffle them, listen to your intuition and let them speak to you.

When you have selected and turned over a card, look at it. Allow the impressions to wash over you; let your intuition speak and images come to you. Then, if you wish to go further, turn to this booklet to read the message and meaning of the card.

Before using this oracle for the first time, you can let it rest on coarse salt for one night (placing the salt on a tissue or thin piece of fabric then throwing out the salt in the morning). Ask the salt to absorb anything negative the oracle might carry. Once the oracle has been purified, connect with it – take the deck into your hands, hold it against your heart chakra and send it love – to create a true energy connection so it may respond perfectly to your requests. Keep the deck wrapped in a piece of fabric or in its bag; you can even place a dried laurel leaf on each side of the box to protect it from any possible negativity. You can also infuse light into the oracle by visualising light inside it, and ask it to be a source of guidance, rightness, peace and healing for you – your body, soul, spirit and feminine – all the subtle dimensions of your being. Finally, imagine that an invisible thread of light connects you to your oracle; this thread is a true heart connection. You can repeat this ritual from time to time, especially if another person has touched or used your oracle, if your oracle has been in a negative environment, if it seems heavy or if you wish to start a new cycle in your life.

DIVINE·ORACLE SPREADS

SIMPLE ONE-CARD SPREAD

Empty your mind, ask a question internally (only one question or intention) and shuffle the cards. Draw one card and, listening to your intuition, let it speak to you. Then turn to this booklet to read about the meaning of the card.

SPECIAL UNDERSTANDING SPREAD

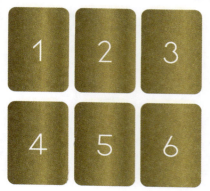

The special understanding spread aims to provide an overview of a situation over a period of at least one month, specifically using the oracle's categories.

Separate the cards into the six categories (using the overview provided on pages 4–5 if you like). Think of your question or intention, shuffle each pack (or category) of cards and draw one card from each pack. Let your intuition speak to you, then turn to this booklet for the meanings of the cards.

SPECIAL EVOLUTION SPREAD

The special evolution spread is good for three months; it includes three cards corresponding to the three coming months so that you may know what to work on during those periods.

Ask a question, set your intention or simply let the cards tell you what you need to hear in the moment. Shuffle the deck, empty your mind and select three cards. Let your intuition speak to you, then turn to this booklet for the meanings of the cards.

SPECIAL DIRECTION SPREAD

The special direction spread lets you know what direction to take for one month; it includes four cards corresponding, respectively, to the four coming weeks. Shuffle the deck, empty your mind and select four cards. Let your intuition speak to you, then turn to this booklet for the meanings of the cards.

When you are finished with the special direction spread, check a lunar calendar for the next new and full moons. Enter into harmony with the moon cycle by engaging with the following points:

- ♥ New moon: create a new cycle; try for renewal; set intentions.
- ♥ Full moon: undertake specific work according to a selected card or release things connected with a selected card.

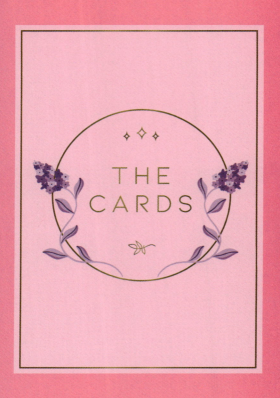

THE

CARDS

THE
AMAZON

1. INDEPENDENT

❧ CATEGORY ❧

RESOURCES AND QUALITIES

*Key words: independence, autonomy, confidence,
strength, instinct, rightness, centring*

You are invited to recognise particular qualities you
possess and develop or strengthen others. If any of these
qualities bother or frighten you, try to understand why – if
you hold fears or memories, or old experiences or beliefs

are being revived set intentions to work on and release these things:

- ♥ You are independent and autonomous. You carry all the resources necessary to be fulfilled. You embrace your destiny without being influenced by others or social conventions.

- ♥ You have confidence in yourself, life and the unseen. Nothing can sway your determination. Life and the universe are your allies, which help you accomplish what you want.

- ♥ You are strong and courageous. You know who you are, you don't look for external validation, your will is boundless and you let no one slow you down or even stop you.

- ♥ You feel connected to nature and can follow your instincts. These instincts confidently guide you and confer great power to your actions. Your connection to nature – animals, plants and minerals – inspires, stimulates and heals you.

- ♥ You are in your own rightness. You are a constant witness to what you truly want, not your fears, lacks or wounds. This alignment enables you to smoothly fulfil your potential.

- ♥ You are centred. You can focus intensely on all that matters to you, which lets you move forward quickly.

Do any of these reminders frighten you? Do any of them awaken anything unpleasant or uncomfortable inside you? If the answer is 'yes', why is that? Ask yourself if it concerns fears, memories, old experiences or unconscious beliefs.

Take time to name these things, then renounce your fears with a loud 'Yes!' Choose to embody the person you are deep inside who you know is there, hidden under layers of fears and negative experiences. From now on, embody this beautiful person in your thoughts, words and actions.

2. THREATENED

THREATENED

❞ CATEGORY ❞

WOUNDS

Key words: danger, terrors, persecution, fear

This card invites you to recognise a wounded self deep inside you.

A wounded self can originate from your past but may also be in your cellular memory through the collective unconscious or ancestral trauma. It may be born from a lack of fulfilment of needs, be they physiological or regarding

security, love, acceptance, validation and recognition. By recognising and healing your wounded self you release emotional pain and conscious and unconscious fears.

GUIDANCE

Inside you there may be a wounded self who has suffered, felt threatened or maybe even been persecuted or felt weak before powerful, ferocious and abusive people.

Your wounded self may have found itself in a delicate position, which made you vulnerable and put you in danger. It may have sacrificed itself too much or given too much of itself to others.

RISKS

You may feel inner rushes of sadness, pessimism or destruction towards yourself or others or, perhaps, a desire for solitude, which will only serve to push you towards excessive introversion. You may find it difficult to open yourself to others and life in general.

HEALING MANTRA

Recite this mantra regularly, until you feel something change inside you:

'I am safe. The world around me is generous and benevolent towards me.'

VISUALISATION

Visualise yourself being safe in the middle of the world. Imagine a warm sun, a peaceful bubble surrounding you; this is pushing away any danger you might have felt, or still feel, by blowing the danger away from you and others like clouds. Repeat this visualisation until you feel joy at being a part of the brotherhood and sisterhood of humanity, that all danger is past and that you're completely at peace with lightness in your heart.

3. EMPOWERED

EMPOWERED

❧ CATEGORY ☙

RELATIONSHIPS, LOVE AND SEXUALITY

Key words: balance, space, boundaries, availability

This card asks you to bring your relationships with yourself and others into balance. Using the points below as a guide, choose something to work on.

FRIENDSHIPS AND/OR LOVE RELATIONSHIPS

- ♥ I maintain healthy relationships with others, without any dominant/dominated or persecutor/victim dynamic and without any strong/weak feeling.

- ♥ I stop mothering my partner. I let them face their responsibilities and fulfil their own needs autonomously.

- ♥ I let my partner be free and remain free myself. I don't possess this other person; they don't belong to me. They don't possess me; I don't belong to them.

- ♥ I focus on myself to take stock of my needs, reconnect with my personality and develop my autonomy. I move away from fusion with my partner.

- ♥ I choose people who respect what I want and leave me space to attain my goals, people who let me express myself and fulfil my own potential.

- ♥ I pay attention to my boundaries and I respect them; I don't abuse them.

- ♥ I choose people because I know that we'll stimulate each other and help each other grow and evolve.

- ♥ I dare to fall in love and surrender to someone trustingly.

- ♥ I am present, welcoming, tender, available and warm hearted.

SEXUALITY

This card invites you to shine a spotlight on your sexuality. Be daring! Be curious and discover, explore, feel and test. Bring joy, freshness and wonder into your sexuality. Get to know your body, your pleasure, either on your own or with a partner. Recognise what you like and what you don't. Forget guilt; make love by engaging your emotions and connecting with your body, not just to fulfil a physical need. Reconnect with your sensuality, letting it express itself in your friendships or love relationships.

4. UNTAMEABLE

UNTAMEABLE

❧ CATEGORY ❧

SHADOWS

Key words: selfishness, obstinacy, recklessness

This card invites you to work on your shadow side. This is the dark part of your being, which expresses itself through negative character traits. Embrace your shadows without judgement, benevolently and lovingly. When you act from darkness part of you is in pain and your ego is setting up protective strategies to preserve you.

GUIDANCE

Reflect upon the traits below in which you recognise yourself; you are invited to regulate excesses in your personality for greater inner peace and joy:

- ♥ You may be too emotionally distant, harsh, aggressive and even pitiless, especially when faced with injustice.

- ♥ You may be too competitive, independent, selfish, obstinate, inflexible or angry. You can also be stubborn because you want to prove yourself and don't want to lose face.

- ♥ You may be too intrepid. You act on impulse, which can put you in danger because you then find yourself in perilous situations.

Do you recognise yourself in any of these traits? If the answer is 'yes', can you recognise why you act this way and what you are trying to protect yourself from?

REMINDERS OF WISDOM

This card reminds you to:

- ♥ Accept your vulnerability, and even show it. Be indulgent and accept what is; it's neither a weakness nor dangerous to be vulnerable. By letting go of some things and dropping your guard you can finally take care of yourself. Take advantage of your vulnerability to reconnect with and develop your creativity.

- ♥ Be gentler with yourself and others. Show compassion by understanding another's point of view, actions or position or what they are experiencing.

- ♥ Recognise the interdependence between human beings, even if it means you need to trust others and recognise the good in them. Accept that others may even help you.

What intentions can you set, or what commitments can you make?

5. GROUNDED

GROUNDED

⚜ CATEGORY ⚜

CHAKRAS

Key words: grounding, presence, connection

This card invites you to connect with your root chakra. Take time to feel where it's located and connect with it, then connect with the ground and feel Mother Earth's energy rise up inside you. Mother Earth can help you and support you.

COUNSEL

1. The following visualisation exercise is to practise grounding. Imagine you're a tree with beautiful roots plunging deep into the earth. The tree is superb, powerful and majestic and its roots are strong. Its branches spread into the wind that plays with its leaves. You feel the shudder of the air; you feel the insects running over your trunk; you feel how much this tree teems with life. Take your time to ground your power. Ground yourself deeply in the earth and feel your sap flowing, the blessing of being part of life, the opportunity of being part of nature.

2. To facilitate this connection with nature and ground yourself, spend time outside in the greatness of the plains or the silence of the forest, on the top of a mountain or the banks of a peaceful lake. Choose a place where the energy seems high, the air is pure and you will feel happy and at peace. You can also take a walk in the sunshine or rain, let the wind play with your hair or feel the grass under your bare feet. Find which places you are drawn to the most.

3. The following visualisation exercise is to boost your root chakra. Take time to connect with your root chakra, then imagine a ruby in that chakra. The ruby is your energetic connection to the earth. It's shining with marvellous dark red colour. It's powerful and is able to draw energy from the ground into your chakra. This energy is flowing and

nourishing you, giving you power and connecting you to Mother Earth. Mother Earth also finds nourishment in your energy. Ask her what her physical and energetic needs are. Maybe she needs love? Gratitude? Or perhaps she would like you to surrender to her by lying down on the ground? Joyfully, give the earth what she needs.

Connect with your ruby often. If you feel it losing its shine, revive its presence and power again. Use your intuition to own this exercise and do it whenever you need.

MANTRA

'I ground myself. I connect with the ground and the earth. I joyfully accept and claim my presence here.'

6. DETERMINED

DETERMINED

❀ CATEGORY ❀

SELF-KNOWLEDGE AND EXPRESSION

Key words: goals, determination, metamorphosis, shamanism

PERSONAL GROWTH

This card invites you to:

- ♥ Set personal goals and aims for your evolution and extension. You need to act, innovate, stray off beaten paths, create your own destiny and attain the heights you desire. Forget your old beliefs: discover other facets of your being; metamorphose into the person you want to be. Now is the time to make changes.

- ♥ Remain focused on your goals. Follow your life path by listening to your intuition, instincts and feelings. Don't let yourself be diverted; you know what is right and good for you.

- ♥ Help other women to metamorphose. You can accompany them and invite them to be part of the powerful and benevolent sisterhood of women. Young women need you; help them give meaning to their destiny by moving forwards, asserting their rights and freeing themselves. When women free themselves it impacts the whole planet – the earth, nature, animals and human beings. Your help is precious; keep faith and move forwards in all confidence.

CHALLENGES FOR YOU

Use your intuition to choose one of these tools or invent one of your own:

- ♥ Set a goal for yourself coming from a deep inner calland follow it to the end.

- ♥ It's time to innovate, to stray off beaten paths and your comfort zone.

- ♥ Work for the protection and defence of rights on earth, such as nature, humans or animals.

SPIRITUAL GROWTH

You need to reconnect with your spirituality and awaken the shaman within you. A shaman is connected with her instincts and hears the calls of nature. She is connected with the elements, plants and animals, her own wild nature and her cycles, especially those associated with the moon.

CHALLENGES FOR YOU

Use your intuition to choose one of these tools or invent one of your own:

- ❤ Take time to communicate with the elements. For instance, you can practise animal telepathy or connect with the energies in minerals.

- ❤ Observe the moon and its cycles: feel its energies and the impact they have on your emotions, thoughts, dreams and feminine cycle.

THE
MATRIARCH

7. LOYAL

LOYAL

⊱ CATEGORY ⊰

RESOURCES AND QUALITIES

Key words: emotions, preservation, loyalty, commitment

You are invited to recognise particular qualities you possess and develop or strengthen others. If any of these qualities bother or frighten you, try to understand why – if you hold fears or memories or old experiences or beliefs are being revived set intentions to work on and release these things:

- ♥ You have emotional intelligence and are connected to your emotions; you can observe, understand and regulate them and turn them into strengths. Regulating your emotions gives you incredible power, self-awareness and self-confidence. Because you also understand others' emotions you can help others understand how they function, shed light on their invisible mechanisms and advise them how to work on themselves.

- ♥ You may have a conservative soul – not by having nostalgia for a bygone past or a puritan attitude but because you keep particular traditions. You observe and take care of sacred objectsand perpetuate ancient traditions that deeply nourish people. You may also simply avoid falling into overconsumption, hyperactivity or the world's too-hasty evolution, which is a dignified and respectable value.

- ♥ You stay loyal to your principles; you're not influenced by or diverted from your values by external demandsbecause you can ally with your deep self. Others may respect and admire you for these qualities, and this gives you strong foundations. Don't hesitate to celebrate your inner marriage to underline this commitment to yourself. Marry yourself, marry life; nurture what matters to you, inside and out. Never neglect yourself in your devotion to others or they will drain you of your energy or take advantage of you without even realising what they are doing.

Do any of these reminders frighten you? Do any of them awaken anything unpleasant or uncomfortable inside you? If the answer is 'yes', why is that? Ask yourself if it concerns fears, memories, old experiences or unconscious beliefs.

Take time to name these things, then renounce your fears with a loud 'Yes!' Choose to embody the person you are deep inside, who you know is there, hidden under layers of fears and negative experiences. From now on, embody this beautiful person in your thoughts, words and actions.

8. UNAPPRECIATED

UNAPPRECIATED

WOUNDS

Key words: low self-esteem, frustration, shame

This card invites you to recognise a wounded self deep inside you.

A wounded self can originate from your past, but may also be in your cellular memory through the collective unconscious or ancestral trauma. It may be born from a lack of fulfilment of needs, be they physiological or regarding

security, love, acceptance, validation and recognition.
By recognising and healing your wounded self you release
emotional pain and conscious and unconscious fears.

GUIDANCE

Inside you there may be a wounded self who has been
betrayed or felt humiliated or unappreciated.

RISKS

You may wish for solitude and feel triggers of anger or
even fits of violence within you.

HEALING MANTRA

Recite this mantra regularly until you feel
something change inside you:

*'My inner riches are divine. Others need not be
aware of them because I feel good about myself. I fully
recognise the indisputable precious value of my being.'*

VISUALISATION

Take slow, deep breaths, then visualise a precious casket
in front of you, including its colour and decorations.
Imagine you are taking the pain you carry related to your
psychological or emotional wounds and placing it in this
casket. Take your time with this ritual: visualise your pain

in a form that speaks to you – clouds or scars, for example – and feel peace as you place it in the casket. Where there was pain, fill the space with pleasant and velvet energies, which you can draw from the sky like a balm. Charge these energies with love, gentleness and appreciation.

9. COMMITTED

~ CATEGORY ~

RELATIONSHIPS, LOVE AND SEXUALITY

Key words: investment, presence, truth

This card asks you to bring your relationships with yourself
and others into balance. Using the points below as a guide,
choose something to work on.

FRIENDSHIPS AND/OR LOVE
RELATIONSHIPS

- ❤ I don't look for people who value or worship me because I don't need adulation. I only need to humbly recognise my own greatness and light.

- ❤ I accept my celibate status because, within me, I have all the qualities I look for in others.

- ❤ I'm capable of fulfilling my own needs; I can feel perfect fullness when alone.

- ❤ I don't need to be someone's wife, partner or girlfriend. Being in a love relationship will not give me greater importance or a special status or is an end unto itself.

- ❤ I stop idealising others and building castles in the sky. I live in the present moment to avoid disappointments.

- ❤ I stop being emotionally dependent. I spend time alone to feel nourished and stimulated.

- ❤ I develop my autonomy.

- ❤ I renounce all forms of violence and stop taking out my frustration on others. Instead, I explore this anger and see what it has to teach me so I may manage, regulate and transform it.

- ❤ I develop personal projects and widen my circle of female friends. I stop focusing on my love relationship.

- ♥ I find the strength to end a relationship in which I no longer feel fulfilled if I've already tried everything I could to make things better.
- ♥ I avoid people who are too airy, immature or prone to lying.

SEXUALITY

This card invites you to change how you relate to sex. Sex is an invitation to discover, play, relax, merge with a partner and explore your pleasure and your partner's. If you believe sex is a duty, this can stem from your past, education or collective memories. It's time to revisit your sexuality so it corresponds with who you are, letting go of all preconceptions about sex, what is good or bad. What matters is for you and your sexuality to be aligned, for you to feel at peace when making love and afterwards, and for your sexuality to benefit all levels of your being.

10. QUARRELSOME

CATEGORY

SHADOWS

Key words: jealousy, conflict, excess

This card invites you to work on your shadow side. This is the dark part of your being, which expresses itself through negative character traits. Embrace your shadows without judgement, benevolently and lovingly. When you act from darkness part of you is in pain and your ego is setting up protective strategies to preserve you.

GUIDANCE

Reflect upon the traits below in which you recognise yourself; you are invited to regulate excesses in your personality for greater inner peace and joy:

- ♥ You may be too possessive, jealous or oppressive. You can feel bad when your partner or your friends spend time with other people. You may also be tempted to spy on your partner.

- ♥ You may tend to engage in toxic relationships, which hurt you, slow you down or are complicated.

- ♥ You may be vindictive, trying to take revenge on or quarrelling with others.

- ♥ You may be touchy and hypersensitive about what others say and how they look at you. You take things too much to heart; you may catastrophise because you feel targeted and hurt, which can lead you to sulk, show anger or feel belittled.

Do you recognise yourself in any of these traits? If the answer is 'yes', can you recognise why you act this way and what you are trying to protect yourself from?

REMINDERS OF WISDOM

This card reminds you to:

- ❤ Give others space and learn to develop trust. If you don't trust others, maybe you lack self-confidence. Does this insecurity stem from a fear of being abandoned, humiliated or rejected, or perhaps you feel you don't deserve to be loved? Instead of remaining in fear, become aware of your qualities; meet them and expand them with gentle and quiet strength so you can be at peace with yourself.

- ❤ Stop hurting yourself, looking unconsciously for toxic relationships to wound yourself or another. Develop your self-esteem to finally meet friendly, benevolent, interesting and especially sincere people. What was your model for human relationships? Release any damaging conditioning and shout a loud 'Yes!' to peaceful and nurturing relationships, which will bring out the best in you. Peaceful relationships don't mean routine and boredom, but gentleness and respect.

- ❤ Find your inner peace. Your relationship with yourself affects your relationships with others. Even if you feel resentment or impulses of anger or revenge, taking it out on others won't make things better. Anger is felt against yourself first, so work on your wounds and free yourself from past traumas by transforming the negative energies that poison your mind and body and bring difficult or even violent situations into your life.

Thenyou'll finally be able to love yourself at your fair value.

- ♥ Show humility sometimes; don't take things literally or personally. If some things strike like an arrow to your heart perhaps you should change your outlook on yourself and your unhealed wounds, which react when someone says something negative to you. Instead of responding hurtfully, be gentle. This will create a protective cocoon around you, which will prevent what others say from resonating with your inner hurts.

What intentions can you set or what commitments can you make?

11. TANTRIC

✦ CATEGORY ✦

CHAKRAS

Key words: sacred sexuality, voluptuousness, experience

This card invites you to connect with your sacral chakra. Stimulate it to increase your vitality as well as discover, explore and practise a form of sacred sexuality.

COUNSEL

1. Feel free and creative in your life, both generally and sexually. Renew yourself, feeling free to explore your sexuality and take paths that call to you. You are a trailblazer: listen to your deep desires and cast aside your doubts and fears. Forget your beliefs or learnings that might lead you to think yourself brazen or that what you do will bother others or make waves. Rely on your senses, intuition and deep desires to confidently reclaim your sexuality for you.

2. Initiate yourself into the realm of conscious sexuality; listen to yourself deeply to guide your partner, practise slow sex and pay attention to your feelings to know what is happening deep within you. Imagine your pubic area is a flower and your sacral chakra is a beautiful, shimmering orange crystal, then feel the whole area open up. Be comfortable with your body and let it express itself during sex like a fluid, intuitive and sacred dance.

3. Try a spiritual experience with sex; explore a sacred union with your partner, feel your connection and the unconditional love that binds you and experience a transcendental act that will fill the energy of your chakras until you reach seventh heaven (the seventh chakra), connecting your body to celestial energy. Your carnal body is a vehicle, letting you access divine dimensions. Accessing these dimensions raises your energies and transforms

humanity's heavy memories regarding sex and male/female abuse, allowing women to find and take their rightful place.

MANTRA

'I stimulate my vital energy for my greater good. My sexuality is moving towards powerful, sacred and alchemical dimensions, which bring me personal and spiritual joy, happiness and satisfaction.'

12. DEVOTED

DEVOTED

❧ CATEGORY ❧

SELF-KNOWLEDGE AND EXPRESSION

*Key words: commitment, well-being,
radiance, partnership, connection*

PERSONAL GROWTH

This card invites you to:

♥ Commit to projects that inspire and resonate with
you and of which you will be proud. Invest yourself
wholly; be thorough and attentive, be a perfectionist,

be conscientious and listen to your heart. Your projects will be filled with positive energy.

- ♥ Make room for your personal and private life; take care of yourself.

- ♥ Help people who need it by bringing them a fresh pair of eyes, encouraging them and showing them benevolence and recognition. Counsel them by listening to your intuition, but even your presence will give them momentum. Still, don't forget to prioritise yourself by nurturing your ambitions, wishes and deepest desires. Using visualisation and positive thoughts and emotions, feel how success is like a bud about to open. Surround this bud with love to infuse and model it on an energetic level.

- ♥ Collaborate with others, establish partnerships and work collectively. We are stronger together and combining ideas with people's skills and energies makes for quicker progress. Keep watch to ensure harmony, understanding and positive communication within the group.

CHALLENGES FOR YOU

Use your intuition to choose one of these tools or invent one of your own:

- ♥ Bring a project to life. Set intentions for a new or existing project, then imagine it growing and expanding. Water it with positive energy, words and light.

- Bring your perspective to a projector offer benevolent energies to another project that needs them.

- Forge ties between people who you feel have things or goals in common.

SPIRITUAL GROWTH

This card invites you to connect the yin and yang inside you, your masculine and feminine energies. Balance and unite their forces to obtain equilibrium. Find what resources you need to flourish and develop your inner completeness; this state of fullness will nourish you to your very cells.

You may be called to shed light on male/female conflicts around you. Send benevolence and positive intentions, and visualise these two energies fully connecting with and embracing each other to overcome and transform ancestral resentment.

CHALLENGES FOR YOU

Use your intuition to choose one of these tools or invent one of your own:

- List which adjectives best define you when you feel yin (feminine) and yang (male) energy. See if they mesh well together or if they collide or conflict. Strive to remedy these imbalances and recover your inner harmony.

❤ Following your intuition, offer to help partners, couples, colleagues or siblings who have trouble cooperating.

THE
CHILD-
WOMAN

13. RECEPTIVE

❦ CATEGORY ❦

RESOURCES AND QUALITIES

Key words: gathering, overcoming, lucidity

You are invited to recognise particular qualities you possess and develop or strengthen others. If any of these qualities bother or frighten you, try to understand why – if you hold fears or memories or old experiences or beliefs are being revived set intentions to work on and release these things:

- You can weave things together, connecting them so they bring you mutual benefits, collaborating, communicating, meshing and nurturing them. You can draw people together (such as finding the right therapist or perfect gift for someone or reconciling people who are at odds) and bridge what concerns you (such as knowing your faults, finding your needs or establishing communication between yourself and a wounded self).

- You are resilient. You can quickly move on to something else, not dwelling on negative situations, and revive momentum when others are giving up. Stay driven by this inner energy whatever happens, and use it to boost yourself and motivate people around you in long-term projects. Use this capacity to overcome obstacles and attain heights; you'll feel the accomplishment and satisfaction of success and completed work.

- You shed light on shadows, and you shine even in the darkest places. You can make a sad person smile again by helping them see the positive in dark situations. Your intuition and psychic abilities let you go still further, because you can explore the depths, emotions and repressed memories in yourself and others, shed light on what is in shadow and grasp fears or unconscious mechanisms to process, regulate, transform and heal them.

Do any of these reminders frighten you? Do any of them awaken anything unpleasant or uncomfortable inside you? If the answer is 'yes', why is that? Ask yourself if it concerns fears, memories, old experiences or unconscious beliefs.

Take time to name these things, then renounce your fears with a loud 'Yes!' Choose to embody the person you are deep inside, who you know is there, hidden under layers of fears and negative experiences. From now on embody this beautiful person in your thoughts, words and actions.

14. ABUSED

※ CATEGORY ※

WOUNDS

Key words: self-pity, victimisation, self-withdrawal

This card invites you to recognise a wounded self deep inside you.

A wounded self can originate from your past but may also be in your cellular memory through the collective unconscious or ancestral trauma. It may be born from a lack of fulfilment of needs, be they physiological or regarding

security, love, acceptance, validation and recognition. By recognising and healing your wounded self you release emotional pain and conscious and unconscious fears.

GUIDANCE

Inside you there may be a wounded self who has experienced trauma or been a victim or felt abused, tormented, alone, helpless, neglected or forgotten.

RISKS

You may tend to withdraw from yourself or feel self-pity or fear towards your own darkness. Repressed thoughts and emotions – such as rage, guilt and powerlessness – can make you passive and malleable, push you into inertia and immobility or make you seem fragile and vulnerable.

HEALING MANTRA

Recite this mantra regularly until you feel something change inside you:

'I recognise my assets and values. I embody them deeply and confidently in peace and harmony.'

VISUALISATION

Imagine a bubble around you. The bubble is protection but also a cocoon, and it responds to your heart's commands through your intention. This bubble shines to protect you and keep negativity away from you. Within the bubble you also shine. You hold yourself straight with shoulders back and head high, proud and dignified, as your aura fills your bubble like a flamboyant and reassuring sun.

15. INDECISIVE

✼ CATEGORY ✼

RELATIONSHIPS, LOVE AND SEXUALITY

Key words: decision, authenticity, wisdom

This card asks you to bring your relationships with yourself and others into balance. Using the points below as a guide, choose something to work on.

FRIENDSHIPS AND/OR LOVE RELATIONSHIPS

- ♥ I make choices in love. I commit to someone; I'm there for them as they are for me. If I fear commitment I'll find out why it panics me and how I can change that.

- ♥ I stop wanting to please others at all costs. I am myself even if I don't conform to others' expectations.

- ♥ I inspire other women to accept and let their femininity shine.

- ♥ I choose stable, reassuring and well-grounded people.

- ♥ I am available to others as they are to me.

- ♥ I reveal myself as a woman, no longer a child. If I tend to show up as a child I'll find out why and what fears are lurking behind this tendency.

- ♥ I create a balance between the time I dedicate to myself and that I offer others, and I am totally present when I am with someone.

- ♥ I dare to do new things, to explore and discover, ensuring these things are deep and not superficial.

SEXUALITY

This card invites you to make your sexuality blossom like springtime; to make it fun, amusing, adventurous and happy. Be sensual in your sexuality, almost hypnotic, without playing manipulative games but awakening the sleeping goddess within. Dare to awaken the energy of kundalini at the base of your spine; be expressive, creative and liberated. Release the sexual passion within, which makes you fully alive (without sliding into too much wildness), free, jovial and happy, like fireworks are bursting inside you. Let your body express itself, undulate, stretch and dance. Listen to your body's intelligence, letting it vibrate and shine, and hear what it has to say and offer.

16. SELF-CENTRED

❧ CATEGORY ☙

SHADOWS

Key words: indecision, selfishness, immaturity, procrastination

This card invites you to work on your shadow side. This is the dark part of your being, which expresses itself through negative character traits. Embrace your shadows without judgement, benevolently and lovingly. When you act from darkness part of you is in pain and your ego is setting up protective strategies to preserve you.

GUIDANCE

Reflect upon the traits below in which you recognise yourself; you are invited to regulate excesses in your personality for greater inner peace and joy:

- ♥ You are indecisive. It's difficult to commit, make decisions and choices or invest in things long term. Like a bee, you forage left and right according to your mood but are unable to offer your presence, time and care to someone or something.

- ♥ You display selfish behaviour. You tend to think about your own comfort and well-being and not consider others' needs and demands. Perhaps you think the world revolves around you or maybe you're narcissistic, sometimes lying and manipulating to get what you want even if you feel guilty about it later.

- ♥ You are disruptive. You sometimes don't notice others' suffering, weariness or fatigue because you can be highly strung and self-centred, boastful and playful like a child with boundless energy. You may do too much and not consider the importance of what others are doing and disrupt them for unimportant and superficial things.

- ♥ You act immaturely. You are like a child-woman stamping her foot and showing impatience when it comes to getting what she wants. You are sometimes capricious, indifferent or sulky when things don't turn out to your advantage or don't happen as you'd like or when someone doesn't keep their promises.

♥ You can procrastinate. You delay your tasks and missions to follow what calls you in the moment or lose yourself in daydreams.

Do you recognise yourself in any of these traits? If the answer is 'yes', can you recognise why you act this way and what you are trying to protect yourself from?

REMINDERS OF WISDOM

This card reminds you to:

♥ Renounce something. By renouncing you leave room for more important things and can put your energy in growing what your heart chooses, which brings great satisfaction. Even if it seems frightening or difficult to choose one course of action because it feels confining or restrictive or you fear success, it's time to express your maturity or know-how by tapping into your abilities to organise, be present, motivate and be dedicated.

♥ Become more altruistic. Consider others' needs and priorities, listen to what they say, take them seriously and help or take care of them without forgetting your own heart and soul.

♥ Learn to settle down. Lower your excess energy when you are highly strung or too agitated to see things clearly so you can redirect that overflowing energy towards your goals and aims or the calling of soul or divine will.

- ♥ Be rigorous and responsible. This isn't boring; responsibility may bring great satisfaction if you take charge of something you care about. Create lists of things to do and do them with joy. Don't push things back to laterand don't flit aimlessly or turn aside from fear of failure.

What intentions can you set or what commitments can you make?

17. FERRYWOMAN

FERRYWOMAN

 CATEGORY

CHAKRAS

Key words: shining, unseen, psychic abilities

This card invites you to connect with your solar plexus chakra, to shine on your surroundings with your entire being and develop and use your psychic potential.

COUNSEL

1. Imagine you are a shining sun, with your rays touching others and illuminating, comforting or stimulating them. Your rays are limitless, free and powerful and nothing can stop them. Dare to be who you are; you will inspire others to do the same, to reveal who they really are and light up what surrounds them too.

2. If you are drawn to psychic phenomena or if these call to you or make you feel curious, now is the time to learn more, become more aware of your psychic abilities or tap into your abilities with greater confidence. You could become a channel to help people receive messages from departed loved ones or simply talk to these people about the existence of the afterlife. Maybe your mission is to be a ferrywoman, helping lost souls find the other side. Feel if this mission calls to you and if signs such as strange phenomena are revealing your calling.

MANTRA

'I shine with my entire being. My contagious light spreads everywhere and in everything, including in the shadows, through which my glittering and radiant brilliance filters.'

18. GUIDE

❧ **CATEGORY** ☙

SELF-KNOWLEDGE AND EXPRESSION

Key words: jollity, initiatives, commitment, renewal

PERSONAL GROWTH

This card invites you to:

♥ Express your inner child, zest for life and carefree
  personality. Your inner child wants to be free from
  obligations and responsibilities; they ask you to divest

yourself of that which encumbers you, weighs on your shoulders or eclipses your inner sun. Careful: this isn't a call to quit everything and be reckless, insouciant or irresponsible but rather to enjoy life amply and freely. Lighten your load, be filled with wonder and invest your energy in soul-enriching things that fill you with joy and lightness. What are your inner child's needs, such as wonder, lightness, play, innocence? How can you respect those needs and avoid telling your inner child to be quiet, hide or disappear? Observe when your inner child can express itself or when you repress it and see how it carves out a place in your adult life.

♥ Invest your energy in decisions and initiatives that are meaningful to you. If you've been hesitating, it's time to take the plunge if you are sure of your choices. For this you must ascertain what you really want, know your desires and strengths; a long-term commitment will bring you many riches and great benefits. Don't be afraid of committing to a path, let alone of feeling imprisoned, hemmed in or blocked because a situation can always evolve. You know how to renew yourself where others might slide into inertia. Dare to invest your energy fully despite the inevitable sacrifices, because it takes time for projects to mature. In the endyou'll reap beautiful fruits. Stay flexible, adaptable and joyful; your joy lets you know if you are still on the right path with the right energy.

♥ Persevere and leave nothing undone. Don't give up and see things through to the end. If you tend to leave projects or tasks unfinished, it's time either to wrap them up or imagine you've erased their traces. If you feel guilty about not finishing, apologise by visualising your new path with the motivation and momentum to finish. Honour your commitments, persevere and don't forget you're investing energy towards your own happiness.

CHALLENGES FOR YOU

Use your intuition to choose one of these tools or invent one of your own:

- ♥ End a situation that is no longer right for you that stifles your inner child, then choose from your heart what your soul is calling.

- ♥ Make a choice that erases other possibilities, then fully invest your energy in that choice.

- ♥ Fix achievable deadlines for your projects.

- ♥ Take stock of times when you didn't see things through to the end and ask yourself why. Do you need to adjust some personality traits? Do you have fears? Find out how you can remedy this tendency for the next time you embark on something, how you can maintain a pure and indefatigable force of momentum and motivation.

- ♥ Make a list of what or who you commit to, sign it and fix an achievable deadline, committing yourself to what must be achieved. Don't turn away from this deadline, whatever it takes, before having achieved your aims.

SPIRITUAL GROWTH

This card appears because you have an important vital potential. You carry the energy of spring within you – the power and magic to make flowers rise out of the earth, nurture seeds, spread roots and make buds blossom. Perhaps you don't tap into this creative power, this impulse of life, or you're not in the right time or place.

CHALLENGES FOR YOU

Use your intuition to choose one of these tools or invent one of your own:

- ♥ Redirect your energy to where it's needed, such as in projects that matter to you.

- ♥ Bring a project to life that you've kept inside you for a long time.

- ♥ Sort out your belongings. Tidy up and clean out a place that needs it, then add a touch of magic to it such as positive energy, a feng shui layout, a spritz of fruity perfume or shades of colour.

- ♥ If you have been lacking in energy lately, it's time to wake up and start moving towards your heart's aspirations again.

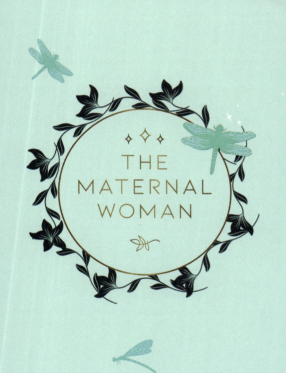

THE
MATERNAL
WOMAN

19. LOVING

✿ CATEGORY ✿

RESOURCES AND QUALITIES

Key words: receptivity, amiability, fertility

You are invited to recognise particular qualities you possess and develop or strengthen others. If any of these qualities bother or frighten you try to understand why – if you hold fears or memories or old experiences or beliefs are being revived set intentions to work on and release these things:

♥ You are receptive. Already, you receive intuitive messages and advice for other people and you can interpret these things. If not, this card tells you to have confidence in yourself, translate what you receive into words and share it. You can also perceive other people's non-explicit, non-verbal requests; pay attention, feel and decode the energies around you and catch things people tend not to see. You perceive in the form of feelings, visions and strong intuitions. Start developing this talent more, validate it and see how it can accompany you and be useful to others.

♥ You are loving. You embrace others as they are, see them as children without judgement, take care of them and lovingly get them to move when needed with patience and total acceptance. You can see others in their beauty, detecting their still-dormant potentials, their light and their souls' greatness. You can also help to encourage others to see who they really areand love, accept and reveal themselves.

♥ You are fertile because you carry and nurture your projects, seeding them with love, patience, positive and constructive thoughts as well as joyful emotions and motivational energies. You can also be a midwife to others, helping people give birth to their projects and taking care and nurturing these projects when they are still embryonic. Your midwifery skills can help to develop the new world. You let the energies of the cosmos flow through you like project ideas coming from the divine without looking to do something about them or give them material form. You even suggest these ideas to people who will know how to accomplish them.

Do any of these reminders frighten you? Do any of them awaken anything unpleasant or uncomfortable inside you? If the answer is 'yes', why is that? Ask yourself if it concerns fears, memories, old experiences or unconscious beliefs.

Take time to name these things, then renounce your fears with a loud 'Yes!' Choose to embody the person you are deep inside, who you know is there, hidden under layers of fears and negative experiences. From now on embody this beautiful person in your thoughts, words and actions.

20. LACKING

LACKING

❦ CATEGORY ❦

WOUNDS

Key words: lack, sadness, confusion

This card invites you to recognise a wounded self deep inside you.

A wounded self can originate from your past but may also be in your cellular memory through the collective unconscious or ancestral trauma. It may be born from a lack of fulfilment of needs, be they physiological or regarding

security, love, acceptance, validation and recognition. By recognising and healing your wounded self you release emotional pain and conscious and unconscious fears.

GUIDANCE

Inside you there may be a wounded self who has lacked maternal love, total acceptance or unconditional generosity.

Your wounded self has suffered from having a mother who was too demanding or removed or perhaps too demonstrative. Someone may have disappointed you; they haven't been there for you even though you have given them a lot.

RISKS

You tend towards disappointment, passiveness and resignation. You may feel your lacks or wants are impossible to fill or that others don't care about you and you are alone. This can make you feel sad, even to the brink of despair.

HEALING MANTRA

Recite this mantra regularly until you feel something change inside you:

'My emotional and vital needs are completely fulfilled by myself, whom I trust and honour. I value my own presence without needing contributions from others even if I appreciate their generosity towards me.'

VISUALISATION

Visualise yourself in a cocoon of energy filled with beauty – perhaps a place to sit or lie down, a special colour, peace-inducing decorations or inspiring symbols. Listen to your intuition and feelings to understand why you choose what beautifies your cocoon if messages or energies come to you from the objects. Imagine a healing mist with positive waves and healing properties filling you and surrounding you. Feel that everything you need is here in this bubble out of time and space; you need nothing else because you have access to fullness, complete bliss, comforting warmth, beneficial energies and infinite love. If you still feel a lack, add things until you are at peace.

21. UNCONDITIONAL

21

UNCONDITIONAL

RELATIONSHIPS, LOVE AND SEXUALITY

Key words: love, giving, boundaries, preservation

This card asks you to bring your relationships with yourself and others into balance. Using the points below as a guide, choose something to work on.

FRIENDSHIPS AND/OR LOVE
RELATIONSHIPS

- ❤ I stop looking for people to mother.
- ❤ I mistrust narcissistic people, who might abuse me and put me down.
- ❤ I assert myself before people who try to mould me to their preference.
- ❤ I manage to say 'no'.
- ❤ I stop waiting for and wanting things from others; I choose people who are available for me.
- ❤ I no longer suffer because of others. I stay distanced from what they experience and I stop dwelling on them and hurting for them.
- ❤ I avoid co-dependent relationships.
- ❤ I avoid immature people.
- ❤ I stop sacrificing myself for others.
- ❤ I stop infantilising others.
- ❤ I avoid overly demanding people, who will empty me of my energy.
- ❤ I am my own best friend. I remain present for myself, and I love being in my own company.

SEXUALITY

This card invites you to infuse your sexual relationships with greater tenderness, affection and gentleness without sliding into being childlike. Choose someone who will listen to your deep needs, who will be gentle and loving with you and with whom you will feel attuned. If your education or beliefs have influenced you into thinking that sex is only for procreation and not for pleasure or that making love is an obligation to satisfy or please your partner, free yourself from these thoughts. Discover how sacred sexuality can be fun and a source of ecstasy while still respecting your connection with your body and emotions.

22. INVASIVE

~ CATEGORY ~

SHADOWS

Key words: jealousy, abuse, rigidity

This card invites you to work on your shadow side. This is the dark part of your being, which expresses itself through negative character traits. Embrace your shadows without judgement, benevolently and lovingly. When you act from darkness part of you is in pain and your ego is setting up protective strategies to preserve you.

GUIDANCE

Reflect upon the traits below in which you recognise yourself; you are invited to regulate excesses in your personality for greater inner peace and joy:

- ♥ You can be possessive. You don't give others enough room to breathe; you invade their vital space, fill up their bubble or breach their intimacy. You tend either to stifle others or expect too much from them.

- ♥ You can be sarcastic and abusive. You can be biting and hurtful, underlining what is amiss rather than what is going well and sometimes disrupting the lives of others when they haven't asked for your help. These people might not be ready for change. You have trouble slowing down when you involve yourself in the lives of others; you tend to stick your nose in everywhere to help but you may overstep the boundaries of their intimacy and hamper their free will.

- ♥ You can try too hard to control everything. You decide things for others because you want to manage everything, or you make choices for others without considering their opinions because you're certain that you're helping them or that you know better than they do.

- ♥ You can be too protective; you mollycoddle others. While you mother them with the best of intentions, you instead prevent them from discovering their own resources, making mistakes and facing reality.

Do you recognise yourself in any of these traits? If the answer is 'yes', can you recognise why you act this way and what you are trying to protect yourself from?

REMINDERS OF WISDOM

This card reminds you to:

- ♥ Let others live their lives freely, even if you feel neglected and alone and want attention, because you might be caring for others to avoid seeing your own wounds and issues.

- ♥ Let others experience what they must because it's not up to you to decide for them. You can't control or shoulder everything. Let go; others must be free to act even if confronted with hardship, because controlling them isn't helping them – they need to learn.

- ♥ Find your own fulfilment in some other way than by having children or by what you bring or give others. You don't need to feel useful to legitimise your existence. You have your own place on earth. Search within yourself and do things that have meaning for you, resonate in you and ally with your own self.

What intentions can you set or what commitments can you make?

23. HEALER

✤ CATEGORY ✤

CHAKRAS

Key words: peace, freedom, care, completeness

This card invites you to connect with your heart chakra.
Allow it to shine, surround and embrace everyone you
meet and let it take care of yourself, others and the whole
world. You don't have to act; simply shine your prolific and
protective energy.

COUNSEL

1. Help others' hearts to be at peace. Help others to forgive and develop values such as brotherhood, sisterhood, mutual assistance and tolerance. Invite people to not judge but be generous and loving towards themselves and the world.

2. This visualisation exercise is to free your heart. Imagine you are freeing your heart from the chains and padlocks that may bind, restrict or imprison it. Free your heart fearlessly, being carried by the wish and right to love freely, widely, unconditionally and for no particular reason – simply because loving makes you happy, fills you with gratitude and satisfies your being. You don't need to know someone or for someone to be part of your life to love them. Love them like a child who is moved by the world, because love is pure, innocent, limitless and without boundaries.

3. Connect with Mother Earth to understand her and receive her energies. Mother Earth supports, nourishes and accepts us as we are. Imagine that you are this planet and that you feel what she experiences – her connection with all her realms, her loving energy flowing through all creation and her fabulous aura and how this connection resembles yours. You can develop your values of ecofeminism by taking care of Mother Earth, because when you take care of her you also take care of creation and nature and your own nature connected to life and love.

MANTRA

'I unreservedly let my heart overflow. I surround the world with positive and benevolent energy and unconditional love. I am free to love and love myself fully, simply and unconditionally with my whole being and grace.'

24. GENEROUS

GENEROUS

✳ CATEGORY ✳

SELF-KNOWLEDGE AND EXPRESSION

*Key words: abundance, generosity,
security, maternity, youthful spirit*

PERSONAL GROWTH

This card invites you to:

♥ Use your ability to create abundance in your life and
the lives of others. By working for things that are right,
that have called you and in which you invest yourself

body and soul, energies will prosper around you. Say a loud 'Yes!' to simplicity and fluidity because things don't need to be difficult or complicated. Everything can be fine and unfold well, and the resources you need may appear suddenlyas if by magic. Don't forget that the divine always works backstage; have faith in the generosity of energy flows and be generous yourself so the law of resonance may operate. If you show generosity your being will radiate it and then attract it in turn.

♥ Express your maternal instincts. You don't need to be a mother to connect with these instincts; the energies of gentleness, maternity and care can bring warmth, security and love to anyone including yourself. You can express these instincts through what you radiate as well as tender gestures, little kindnesses, pleasant words, kind looks and sincere smiles.

♥ Show youthful spirit – allow new ideas to burgeon inside you and your creativity to express itself by showing generosity, having a novel and fresh outlook, letting yourself be filled with childlike wonder and sparkling with happiness. Bring dynamism where people and situations appear to stagnate and energy no longer flows. Your freshness of spirit can be a magic wand waved into bleak places or situations, bringing youth, renewal, brightness, liveliness and energy into things, people and situations.

CHALLENGES FOR YOU

Use your intuition to choose one of these tools or invent one of your own:

- ❤ Visualise abundance all around you. Dare to dream big with your heart, not your ego, so things may manifest. Imagine and feel that benefits can come to you from everywhere and surround you. Create and receive abundance for yourself or for others if you are involved in other people's projects. Boost or help people to manifest what their souls need to fulfil their potential.

- ❤ Invest yourself in a nutrition project to create a world in which food is healthy, vibrant, nourishing, natural and joyful. You can do this in the fields or kitchen or through good advice, as long as it brings a new awareness, outlook or elevated energy into this area.

- ❤ Dust off a situation that needs brightening or boosting. Take things into your own hands to sort or tidy them or bring freshness, energy, colours, ideas and motivation.

SPIRITUAL GROWTH

This card appears because you can offer your support to others, accompany them calmly and optimistically and nourish them spiritually.

Your counsel is more precious than it might appear. When you listen to your intuition or your soul your counsel is vibrant and right. You can connect the seen and unseen to encourage people to listen to repressed parts of their beings because of wounding or childhood trauma. Listen to these people and care for them lovingly and patiently to help them and guide them towards greater spirituality and self-knowledge.

CHALLENGES FOR YOU

Use your intuition to choose one of these tools or invent one of your own:

- ♥ Accompany someone as they explore their shadows. You could encourage that person to see a therapist, or counsel them by listening to your intuition if you feel this information is right and congruent and the person is capable of receiving it.

- ♥ Spend time exploring your inner world through meditation and visualisations and by paying attention to your feelings.

- ♥ Paint intuitively. Focus on your inner belly to connect with your depths, then paint following your intuitionwithout trying to create anything pretty, just painting in a way that inspires you (for instance, painting with a brush, finger or sponge). Observe your work and feel what it is trying to tell you.

THE
SENSUAL
WOMAN

25. ALCHEMIC

ALCHEMIC

※ CATEGORY ※

RESOURCES AND QUALITIES

Key words: transformation, transcendence, magic

You are invited to recognise particular qualities you possess and develop or strengthen others. If any of these qualities bother or frighten you try to understand why – if you hold fears or memories or old experiences or beliefs are being revived set intentions to work on and release these things:

♥ You transform lead into gold. Like a fairy with a magic wand you can bring lightness where things seem heavy, joy where there is sadness and light where there is shadow or darkness. Use this power to beautify your own life but also to bring positive energy where it's right and needed, by offering a sincere smile, giving advice, adding colour or playing festive music. But take care not to slide into saviour syndrome or co-dependency.

♥ You know your strengths and express them. You aren't ashamed of showing and expressing your qualities or being in the spotlight. You don't fear judgement, jealousy or being criticised. You are proud of your aptitudes or character traits that let you fulfil your potential and even know success in society or at work. Your qualities may help you succeed at tasks or carry out wonderful projects for yourself – ambitious projects that may inspire others.

♥ You use your polarities to inspire your actions such as being gentle and delicate but also cheerful and dynamic. You can rough things out and pay attention to detail and you can stay focused and assiduous, as well as being light and detached. Don't hesitate to play with these polarities in your personal projects, collective endeavours or relationships. Sway joyfully, and enjoy expressing your polarities in harmony and balance.

Do any of these reminders frighten you? Do any of them awaken anything unpleasant or uncomfortable inside you? If the answer is 'yes', why is that? Ask yourself if it concerns fears, memories, old experiences or unconscious beliefs.

Take time to name these things, then renounce your fears with a loud 'Yes!' Choose to embody the person you are deep inside, who you know is there, hidden under layers of fears and negative experiences. From now on embody this beautiful person in your thoughts, words and actions.

26. UNRECOGNISED

UNRECOGNISED

✤ CATEGORY ✤

WOUNDS

Key words: invisibility, transparency, effacement

This card invites you to recognise a wounded self deep inside you.

A wounded self can originate from your past but may also be in your cellular memory through the collective unconscious or ancestral trauma. It may be born from a lack of fulfilment of needs, be they physiological or regarding

security, love, acceptance, validation and recognition. By recognising and healing your wounded self you release emotional pain and conscious and unconscious fears.

GUIDANCE

Inside you there may be a wounded self who has been ignored or scorned by others. Your wounded self hasn't mattered enough to some people and has been overlooked, neglected or unconsidered.

RISKS

You may feel anxiety, emotional fluctuation and a lack of legitimacy. You may fear not mattering to others, not being noticed or recognised, being forgotten or not having your own place.

HEALING MANTRA

Recite this mantra regularly until you feel something change inside you:

'I truly am, and I truly exist. My place is here on earth; I recognise the legitimacy of my presence. I am reassured because I know I exist and matter to myself and also to others without effort.'

VISUALISATION

Each time you feel unrecognised and pushed aside, each time others don't honour your presence or recognise your qualities, imagine a small candle lighting up in every cell of your body. These candles become a bubble of light within and then all around you. Visualise the sun's rays shining on you and mirroring your bubble. Feel your connection with the sun, brilliant and perfectly synchronised. Recognise that you are a shining heavenly body; savour the simple fact of existing and shining in your own eyes.

27. INSPIRING

RELATIONSHIPS, LOVE AND SEXUALITY

Key words: inspiration, expression, maturity, sensuality

This card asks you to bring your relationships with yourself and others into balance. Using the points below as a guide, choose something to work on.

FRIENDSHIPS AND/OR LOVE RELATIONSHIPS

- ❤ I favour monogamous relationships if I tend towards polyamory.

- ❤ I am authentic and stop playing a role to appeal or seduce; I dare to show myself as I truly am.

- ❤ I express my emotions and honour them however suits me best and inspires me.

- ❤ I surround myself with people who are charismatic but not megalomaniacs.

- ❤ I am wary of short-term passions and invest myself in relationships that seem beautiful to me.

- ❤ I stop lying to myself when a new relationship begins because I can say goodbye and have closure even before it starts if I know where it will end.

- ❤ I avoid sexist people and chauvinistic men.

- ❤ I show sentimental stability by releasing the feeling that stability means being trapped in routine.

- ❤ I try to regulate my volatility.

- ❤ I work in the service of love, grace and beauty.

- ❤ I am honest with others; I refrain from lying and using platitudes. I am true.

SEXUALITY

This card invites you to be more sensual, explore your five senses and play with everything while remaining genuine and true. When you make love, drop your masks, bare yourself and show yourself as you truly are without doubt or fear. Be playful and authentic. Have fun; let your inspiration express itself through pleasant and languorous games, which will develop even greater closeness with your partner. Your mind is quick, your body vibrant. Awaken your inner muse, fully revealing yourself to your partner, being natural and spontaneous. Invite art into your sexuality by looking at paintings, listening to music, making pottery or doing body painting. Your body is an instrument in the service of pleasure, but also a work that inspires those who contemplate it.

28. SEDUCTIVE

≫ CATEGORY *≪*

SHADOWS

Key words: impulsiveness, manipulation, games, excess

This card invites you to work on your shadow side. This is the dark part of your being, which expresses itself through negative character traits. Embrace your shadows without judgement, benevolently and lovingly. When you act from darkness part of you is in pain and your ego is setting up protective strategies to preserve you.

GUIDANCE

Reflect upon the traits below in which you recognise yourself; you are invited to regulate excesses in your personality for greater inner peace and joy:

- 💙 You can be too impulsive. You can act without thinking, carried away by your passions, and you sometimes regret your actions or excesses. You may not realise the consequences of your actions, and you may be stubborn even if hearing you were in the wrong.

- 💙 You can be manipulative and seductive, using your magnetic power to charm, because when you do you get what you want. You seduce to win favours, consciously or unconsciously, to obtain support, achieve your goals or even to be loved.

- 💙 You can be too extroverted. Everyone knows when you're somewhere; no one can escape your presence. For instance, you may talk too loudly, gesture wildly, move incessantly or constantly grab attention.

Do you recognise yourself in any of these traits? If the answer is 'yes', can you recognise why you act this way and what you are trying to protect yourself from?

REMINDERS OF WISDOM

This card reminds you to:

- ♥ Listen to your deep feelings and your inner wisdom before speaking up, acting or following your impulses. Be aware of the consequences of your actions and apologise to those you offend when your excessive behaviour injures or wearies them.

- ♥ Observe the moments when you seduce or manipulate others to your advantage, even if it seems inconsequential and you think it doesn't hurt them. To defuse that way of being, be honest with yourself and others, expressing your expectations and needs clearly instead of hypnotising your audience to serve your own interests. Remember: you are likeable without having to overdo it. Others will help you if they think it's right and you can give back in balance.

- ♥ Remember you matter and exist for others without needing to be expansive all the time. Even when you are silent, discreet, calm and inwardly connected your presence can be felt – your essence or energy shines. Learn to leave room for others; your presence is pleasant and important without needing to overdo it.

What intentions can you set or what commitments can you make?

29. EXPRESSIVE

EXPRESSIVE

❧ CATEGORY ❧

CHAKRAS

Key words: beauty, magic, expression

This card invites you to connect with your throat chakra. Express who you are in the deepest part of your being and express yourself as a spiritual being or soul.

COUNSEL

1. Express the most beautiful facets of yourself through what you love most such as dancing, singing, drawing,

gardening or cooking. Choose something that captures your uniqueness, values and your whole light. Free your creativity because nothing is preventing you or holding you back, so unveil and express each of your true nature's light-filled and divine facets.

2. Connect with your inner magic and even with fairyland, then maintain that connection. Notice your daily life's magical details, express your creativity and natural talents and stay sparkling and positive. You could visualise a magical garden inside you, peopled with extraordinary creatures.

3. This visualisation exercise is to free your throat chakra. Imagine a beautiful blue light shining from inside your throat, infusing your entire being and overflowing around you. Let your mouth relax, as chains fall away from your hands and body. Allow yourself to express, create, be present and expand who you are. Let inspiration come. Express yourself in a way that calls to you in a festive atmosphere. Listen to yourself and show what you feel without restraint, in perfect freedom and the right momentum.

> ### MANTRA
>
> *'I rightly express all the light-filled facets of my personality. I express my creativity; it inspires and invigorates me and the world around me.'*

30. CREATIVE

⚹ CATEGORY ⚹

SELF-KNOWLEDGE AND EXPRESSION

*Key words: spontaneity, creativity, renewal,
opportunities, mindfulness*

PERSONAL GROWTH

This card invites you to:

♥ Be creative. You have a talent, perhaps still hidden
or already revealed, teeming inside you just waiting
to be expressed in the service of grace and beauty.

You don't need to intellectualise this talent, only to release it freely, spontaneously, forgetting all constraints. There's no need to apply yourself or reach a goal; simply express the impulse you feel, your heart's aspirations and desires. Create without a particular reason, expectation or judgement. Work naturally and lightly, staying confident; your creativity will free itself wonderfully.

♥ Reinvent yourself or invite others to do so. Leave the past behind you and respond to the flow that calls to you, remembering that magic operates when you're confident and when you surrender to the universe joyfully and unrestrainedly. Take this time to observe whether doors are opening for you – if opportunities are presenting themselves in your work, finances or relationship – to create and manifest a life that is completely you, meeting the calls of your soul and your deepest impulses. Staying allied with your intuitive creativity will help you bring a new world to life and help women to create new professions and ways of doing thingswithout needing past or habitual labels.

♥ Enjoy the present moment by taking time to enjoy life's small pleasures consciously, moderately and rightly. Simply appreciate and savour what is. Feel the elements fire, air, water and earth around you and inside you in what you eat and what you see. Then connect with your senses and feel immense gratitude for what they perceive.

CHALLENGES FOR YOU

Use your intuition to choose one of these tools or invent one of your own:

- ♥ Create intuitively and spontaneously, without looking for a particular result or perfection, and with joy and letting go. Connect with your creation and feel what it expresses to you.

- ♥ Dare to say 'yes' to new things. Seize opportunities that present themselves or imagine your own way of doing something specific, such as reinterpreting a usual recipe, healing energy treatment, song or use of an object.

- ♥ Make a list of things for which you feel grateful such as people you feel lucky to know, songs you love and dishes you adore.

- ♥ Develop your mindfulness. Whether you are vacuuming or taking a walk, be in the present moment; feel things without letting your thoughts take over or analysing anything. Be fully here and now.

SPIRITUAL GROWTH

This card appears because you have creative power in material objects – you can make answers to your needs appear swiftly for your spiritual fulfilment. If you want something truly and deeply, with your whole heart and soul, you have the energy and determination to make what you want manifest quickly.

CHALLENGES FOR YOU

Use your intuition to choose one of these tools or invent one of your own:

- ♥ Write a list of things that are necessary to your personal and spiritual growth or that will help you realise your potential. Then, with every fibre of your being, maintain the intention to see these things appear in reality in the form of opportunities, gifts or something else.

- ♥ Use the power of visualisation to help you manifest something that is essential to you, something you want more than anything, taking care that the call comes from your soul and not your ego.

- ♥ Cast aside anything that is contrary to or might hinder your realisation or fulfilment or the manifestation of your soul's desires. For this, take time to define these things then visualise yourself saying 'no' to them sincerely, moving them aside and replacing them with luminous energies.

THE
ACCOMPLISHED
WOMAN

31. WISE

WISE

❧ CATEGORY ❧

RESOURCES AND QUALITIES

Key words: comprehension, maturity, perspective

You are invited to recognise particular qualities you possess and develop or strengthen others. If any of these qualities bother or frighten you try to understand why – if you hold fears or memories or old experiences or beliefs are being revived set intentions to work on and release these things:

- ♥ You are rational and logical. You can create and establish strategies to bring projects to life, respond to your desires, manage your life differently or help others. Your pragmatic side lets you get straight to the point; you're not plagued by hesitation and you make plans quickly. Your strong and powerful inner impulses help you to act quickly or help others.

- ♥ You are shrewd and reasonable, preferring to observe before acting or speaking. Your self-assurance is such that it counsels, reasons and convinces anyone. You can be influential because people trust you and rely on your wisdom when they need a clear, defined and uplifting direction.

- ♥ You are disciplined and patient, relying on your intellect by harnessing it to your projects. Whatever happens, if you get involved stay the course. Remain committed and resolute even if everything seems to crumble or go wrong or if others jump ship. Through your observation, acumen and sharp analysis you can remodel things if needed to get them back on track or give them a new twist.

- ♥ You preserve yourself. Your natural ability for emotional distance helps you shield yourself from the outside world and remain in touch with your inner self. Especially you don't let yourself be destabilised, offended or weakened by acquaintances or people close to you. You can remain centred despite the frequent demands of the outside world.

Do any of these reminders frighten you? Do any of them awaken anything unpleasant or uncomfortable inside you? If the answer is 'yes', why is that? Ask yourself if it concerns fears, memories, old experiences or unconscious beliefs.

Take time to name these things, then renounce your fears with a loud 'Yes!' Choose to embody the person you are deep inside, who you know is there, hidden under layers of fears and negative experiences. From now on embody this beautiful person in your thoughts, words and actions.

32. ABANDONED

❧ CATEGORY ☙

WOUNDS

Key words: lack, uncertainty, solitude

This card invites you to recognise a wounded self deep inside you.

A wounded self can originate from your past but may also be in your cellular memory through the collective unconscious or ancestral trauma. It may be born from a lack of fulfilment of needs, be they physiological or regarding

security, love, acceptance, validation and recognition. By recognising and healing your wounded self you release emotional pain and conscious and unconscious fears.

GUIDANCE

Inside you there may be a wounded self who has lacked a reassuring and comforting maternal presence who would have passed down matriarchal values to you. Your wounded self may have faced responsibilities when you were too young and should have been enjoying the carefree pleasures of childhood. Too often you found yourself alone without anyone to understand, listen to and support you.

RISKS

You may fear silence and monotony, tend towards disappointment or sadness or feel a lack or inner emptiness that's difficult to fill, a kind of discontent.

HEALING MANTRA

Recite this mantra regularly until you feel something change inside you:

'I am supported and surrounded. I give others the space they need to envelop and accompany me in my life gently, delicately and divinely.'

VISUALISATION

Imagine you're cuddled up in half of someone's heart. Even if that heart is unknown to you, you feel its warmth, its reassuring and comforting love. The heart forges ties with you; it's happy and feels complete and lucky to have you within it. You feel a warm energy, nurturing and mothering like a delicious cocoon – a loving, caring and attentive mother's belly.

33. REASONED

› 33 ‹

REASONED

❧ CATEGORY ❧

RELATIONSHIPS, LOVE AND SEXUALITY

Key words: wisdom, peace, reason

This card asks you to bring your relationships with yourself and others into balance. Using the points below as a guide, choose something to work on.

FRIENDSHIPS AND/OR LOVE RELATIONSHIPS

- ❤ I surrender to reason when I feel my heart's and ego's desires but know these desires would lead me irremediably to disaster.
- ❤ I listen to my heart if my ego tries to block me because of fears.
- ❤ I choose ambitious partners who put themselves in successful situations or who are animated by and passionate about projects that drive them.
- ❤ I stop trying to tame, quieten or set boundaries for others.
- ❤ I make friends with girls and I develop sisterhood. I feel the peacefulness, joy, gentleness and liveliness that this brings.
- ❤ I avoid people who are too dreamy or idealistic, who fabricate, whose heads are in the clouds or who tend towards inertia.
- ❤ I listen to and express my feelings and emotions.

SEXUALITY

This card invites you to see the fun and playful aspect of sexuality and to appreciate the lightness of sex even within its spiritual dimension. Be romantic by lighting candles, playing sensual music and scattering rose petals.

Savour voluptuousness by enjoying sensory pleasures, letting yourself just be and resonating in the grace and beauty of the present moment. Learn to surrender with trust; guide your partner languorously or let yourself be guided while staying perfectly relaxed.

34. DEMANDING

～ CATEGORY ～

SHADOWS

Key words: detachment, obstinacy, judgement, control

This card invites you to work on your shadow side. This is the dark part of your being, which expresses itself through negative character traits. Embrace your shadows without judgement, benevolently and lovingly. When you act from darkness part of you is in pain and your ego is setting up protective strategies to preserve you.

GUIDANCE

Reflect upon the traits below in which you recognise yourself; you are invited to regulate excesses in your personality for greater inner peace and joy:

- ♥ You can be too detached from or lack compassion for other people and situations. You refuse to create ties and be attached. You prefer to remain individual; you aren't there for others because you struggle to truly involve yourself with them or take a place in their lives.

- ♥ You can be obstinate, stubborn and close minded and sometimes too arrogant. You sometimes act without thinking and impulsively reject people who try to take their time. You have trouble asking for forgiveness or reconsidering your actions and you don't like thinking about or questioning what you've done.

- ♥ You can be too critical. You pass hasty judgements and you tend to observe everything to see what can be fixed or improved.

- ♥ You can be too rigid. You lack spontaneity, flexibility and submission. Perhaps change is difficult for you; you prefer to plan and carry things out as you've always done. This reassures you because you like to control things to prevent them from escaping you.

Do you recognise yourself in any of these traits? If the answer is 'yes', can you recognise why you act this way and what you are trying to protect yourself from?

REMINDERS OF WISDOM

This card reminds you to:

- ♥ Connect more with your emotions by dwelling more in your heart and less in your head. When you act, remain in touch with your inner self.

- ♥ Take care of your inner child by playing, feeling, remaining carefree, letting go and slowing down. Connect your body and mind; they'll tell you when it's time to stop and be gentle with yourself. Don't wait until you're wounded or ill to slow down.

- ♥ Stop judging others, be understanding and accept people and situations as they are, even if they seem imperfect to you. Forgive yourself and others easily.

- ♥ Be flexible, open minded and available to receive advice, opinions or criticism from the outside world when it is constructive and benevolent.

What intentions can you set or what commitments can you make?

35. PSYCHIC

✦ CATEGORY ✦

CHAKRAS

Key words: clairvoyance, clarity, lucidity

This card invites you to connect with your third eye chakra to develop and use your clairvoyance. Clairvoyance helps you to be discerning and lucid, to see things clearly.

COUNSEL

1. Remove your filters to see things or people as they truly are; you won't be duped by your beliefs, fears or preconceptions or conditioning or certainties. For this new outlook, imagine you are a child discovering the world without any preconceptions. This child relies on their feelings and knows there is something greater than them. This child does not judge and has no knowledge of social restrictions or other people's expectations.

2. Open your mind and broaden your awareness by developing your higher cosmic mind. Test states of deep meditation: visualise your third eye in the middle of your forehead opening like a skylight to perceive the stars, and feel how this eye can see everywhere all the way up to the heavens. Train yourself to perceive things with your eyes closed and then pay attention to your feelings to decode people, animals and objects.

MANTRA

'My discernment and lucidity let me see things wisely.
Instantaneous, brilliant insights light my way.'

36. WARRIOR

WARRIOR

❧ CATEGORY ❧

SELF-KNOWLEDGE AND EXPRESSION

Key words: calm, wisdom, influence, momentum, strength

PERSONAL GROWTH

This card invites you to:

💜 Keep your composure, remain calm in complex or deteriorating situations and find solutions to restore order or harmony. Listen to yourself so you can set up things one after the other, methodically and pragmatically. You can be agile and manage events tactfully. You are determined and diligent, proactive and productive.

- Keep your cool. This lets you have some perspective when you feel attacked instead of feeling judged or criticised. This helps you to remain focused on what you want rather than on external threats, creating a protective shield around you, letting no one hinder or erase your projects.

- Be wise and reasonable. You give good advice and occupy important positions in society, your words, advice and very presence influencing people in high places.

CHALLENGES FOR YOU

Use your intuition to choose one of these tools or invent one of your own:

- Temper yourself instead of reacting immediately. When strong emotions arise, take deep breaths to channel them and remain in observation rather than reaction. Listen to your inner wisdom.

- Act now. Dare to take important steps to bring projects you care about to life.

- Boldly take your place in a difficult or overwhelming environment. Shine who you are without trying to impose; take your place by letting your presence be known.

SPIRITUAL GROWTH

This card appears because there is a wise and aligned warrior-woman inside you who leaps forward and reasons with men, bringing them out of their constraints and dogmas to participate in a new social awareness. Keeper of wisdom teachings, you can guide anyone who wishes it, anyone who wants to open themselves to a more sacred dimension of life and its mysteries, especially to what is unseen and intangible. Your faith reinforces your protective aura to the outside world, letting you remain connected to your higher self, your consciousness and elevated mind.

CHALLENGES FOR YOU

Use your intuition to choose one of these tools or invent one of your own:

- ♥ Embark on a project or activity that has meaning and is aligned with your soul because it can help the world to change and evolve towards greater wisdom and consciousness.

- ♥ Undertake a rite of initiation or shamanic experience; explore wise teachings that open the mind and broaden awareness; discover the energies all around you in your own way.

- ♥ Reinforce your faith and shine your aura by practising meditation, doing energy exercises or praying.

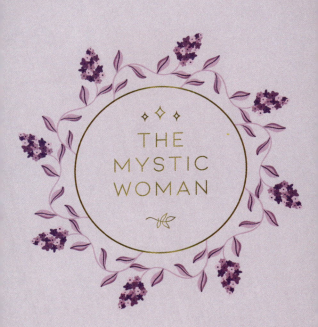

THE
MYSTIC
WOMAN

37. PEACEFUL

PEACEFUL

✢ CATEGORY ✢

RESOURCES AND QUALITIES

Key words: impeccability, warmth, greatness

You are invited to recognise particular qualities you possess and develop or strengthen others. If any of these qualities bother or frighten you try to understand why – if you hold fears or memories or old experiences or beliefs are being revived set intentions to work on and release these things:

- ♥ You remain virginal, pure and intact – in the sense of being unpolluted and unsoiled by the outside world – from the agitation and frenzy of others. Calm and peace abide within you because you are connected to your inner self. Whatever the changes, movements and cycles around you, you are imperturbable, unchangeable and in complete harmony with yourself because you are deeply connected to your essence.

- ♥ You are warm, welcoming, generous, altruistic and attentive and know how to take care of others. You prefer connecting to people you are with, listening to them and lifting their spirits, ensuring everyone feels good instead of being in competition or confrontation.

- ♥ You are serene and solitary. Your contemplative, tranquil and impassive nature and your calm and peaceful character stem from your connection to your inner self. You can regulate your thoughts and emotions; you remain queen of your inner realm and you find your fullness and completeness in your connection to your deep essence. While you appreciate the presence of others you prefer solitude; you feel good in your own company.

Do any of these reminders frighten you? Do any of them awaken anything unpleasant or uncomfortable inside you? If the answer is 'yes', why is that? Ask yourself if it concerns fears, memories, old experiences or unconscious beliefs.

Take time to name these things, then renounce your fears with a loud 'Yes!' Choose to embody the person you are deep inside, who you know is there, hidden under layers of fears and negative experiences. From now on embody this beautiful person in your thoughts, words and actions.

38. NEGLECTED

~⋙ CATEGORY ⋘~

WOUNDS

Key words: lacking, devaluation, insipidness

This card invites you to recognise a wounded self deep inside you.

A wounded self can originate from your past but may also be in your cellular memory through the collective unconscious or ancestral trauma. It may be born from a lack of fulfilment of needs, be they physiological or regarding

security, love, acceptance, validation and recognition. By recognising and healing your wounded self you release emotional pain and conscious and unconscious fears.

GUIDANCE

Inside you there may be a wounded self who has lacked affection, especially maternal love, who has been cast aside and ignored by people who were close or mattered to you.

RISKS

You may feel unworthiness, unappreciation and even shame. You may sometimes feel lost without knowing who you truly are; perhaps you ignore your aspirations, dreams or wishes.

HEALING MANTRA

Recite this mantra regularly until you feel something change inside you:

'My essence is unalterable. I am worthy of love and attention. I am sure of myself. I recognise the energies of love and peace within me, which surround me divinely to bring me happiness and confidence and aid my revelation.'

VISUALISATION

Visualise yourself standing tall with your back and shoulders straight, chin up and feet grounded into the earth. You are in your rightful place; you feel this in your heart and through your entire body. You are surrounded by a ring of people; you may or may not know them or perhaps you only see their outlines. These people send you love, warmth and positive and beneficial energies. You feel these luminous energies are increasingly divine, first touching your skin then enveloping your body, your cells and even the heart of your cells. You are nourished by this bubble of love, grounding it deeply inside you. This bubble is a revitalising and protective cocoon in which you feel in your rightful place – safe, calm, worthy and loved.

39. SOLITARY

SOLITARY

❧ CATEGORY ❧

RELATIONSHIPS, LOVE AND SEXUALITY

Key words: encounter, calm, isolation

This card asks you to bring your relationships with yourself and others into balance. Using the points below as a guide, choose something to work on.

FRIENDSHIPS AND/OR LOVE RELATIONSHIPS

- ♥ I go out, see sociable people and interact with them; I am connected and at ease with the outside world.

- ♥ I radiate warmth and light towards others.

- ♥ I stop choosing people who oppose me unless they complement me.

- ♥ I choose friends or spiritual partners who know how to listen and with whom I can have deep, meaningful discussions.

- ♥ I choose to spend time alone. I withdraw from the world when I need to establish or deepen my connections with my inner self.

- ♥ I am more demonstrative with others.

- ♥ I am never the slave of others; I assert myself benevolently and with composure.

- ♥ I avoid demeaning people; I choose those who value me or spotlight my qualities.

SEXUALITY

This card invites you to feel pleasure, have orgasms and know ecstasy. You can give yourself pleasure alone, such as spending one-on-one time with yourself – you'll feel how you are connected with the force of love and your own inner self – or you can use sex to bond with your partner and benefit from their warmth. Don't hesitate to take things into your own hands. Take the reins and suggest what you like – without trying to dominate your partner or fearing they might otherwise go elsewhere but simply to have fun initiating things.

40. WILD

WILD

↜ CATEGORY ↞

SHADOWS

Key words: antisocial, killjoy, manipulation, docility

This card invites you to work on your shadow side. This is the dark part of your being, which expresses itself through negative character traits. Embrace your shadows without judgement, benevolently and lovingly. When you act from darkness part of you is in pain and your ego is setting up protective strategies to preserve you.

GUIDANCE

Reflect upon the traits below in which you recognise yourself; you are invited to regulate excesses in your personality for greater inner peace and joy:

- ❤ You are sometimes antisocial. It may be difficult to have a social life; you can be shy, introverted and solitary. Through being enough for yourself you may have cut yourself off from others, from going out, meeting people and seeing friends. You may think that the world has nothing to offer you since all the riches, resources and answers to your expectations are already inside you.

- ❤ You are sometimes passive. You can be too docile, submissive or easily influenced. Your lack of assertion and ambition may lead you into toxic relationships with people who take advantage of you or enslave, dominate, manipulate or eclipse you.

Do you recognise yourself in any of these traits? If the answer is 'yes', can you recognise why you act this way and what you are trying to protect yourself from?

REMINDERS OF WISDOM

This card reminds you to:

- ♥ Remember that the outside world can be profitable for you, nourishing and bringing you many benefits. These benefits may not seem vital but they are pleasant, enjoyable and fascinating without disrupting your balance and inward connection.

- ♥ Assert yourself and your personality, opening yourself to others by sharing your tastes, values and aspirations with them. Set yourself personal aims that correspond to your values, showing who you are and establishing your presence. This will let you offer your light to the world, to shine and scatter your beautiful energies so others may benefit from them.

What intentions can you set or what commitments can you make?

41. ORACLE

ORACLE

❧ CATEGORY ☙

CHAKRAS

Key words: presence, cosmic connection, mysticism

This card invites you to spread the energy of your third eye chakra and open yourself up to extrasensory perceptions. Develop your presence and connection to the self and prepare to receive insights and become a guide for others.

COUNSEL

1. Practise mindfulness; stay in the present moment by taking your time to do things. Pay attention to your movements, feelings, surroundings and what your senses tell you; adjust your thoughts and feel complete in the now and grateful for what is.

2. Develop your extrasensory abilities; take the time to perceive and decode the world beyond appearances by connecting to the essence of things – to their energy and what they resonate. By paying attention to messages of clairaudience you may receive auditory messages, brilliant insights, visions, flashes, motifs or symbols. You may even receive impressions of people, objects and situations.

3. Train yourself to listen to your higher consciousness by connecting and referring to it when you make decisions, orient yourself or do anything particular. Develop the part of you that knows, is wise and makes the best decisions for your heart and soul – even if you need to work on your ego, abandon the pastand transform your memories and beliefs.

MANTRA

'My extrasensory perceptions are developing. I feel the energetic essence of things.'

42. ALIGNED

ALIGNED

꘏ CATEGORY ꘏

SELF-KNOWLEDGE AND EXPRESSION

Key words: rightness, verticality, listening to yourself, alignment

PERSONAL GROWTH

This card invites you to:

♥ Focus on one thing at a time, take your time and apply yourself to carry out your tasks. When centred in your heart you can listen to it without giving in to the calls of the outside world. Remain focused on what really matters to you because you can dominate your impulses.

- Remain serene, congenial and warm; you are good at welcoming people and creating a pleasant atmosphere and harmonious environment. Take care of your home and those who live there – your home is like your temple so people should feel good there.

- Be at peace; you aren't particularly materialistic or power hungry. Your inner life can be rich and fertile, especially through meditation and bodywork, because these practices make you feel good and stay connected with your inner self.

CHALLENGES FOR YOU

Use your intuition to choose one of these tools or invent one of your own:

- Apply yourself, not rushing those things you might tend to botch or do too quickly such as getting yourself ready or carrying out routine tasks.

- Take care of yourself, another person or a place if your heart tells you to do so and you think it's worthwhile.

- Develop your connection with your inner self by distancing yourself from the outside world when you need to.

SPIRITUAL GROWTH

This card reminds you that you have great intuition and are able to perceive the essence of people and situations beyond appearances. Generally, you are in an extrasensory state; you can receive intangible information precisely. Always in search of meaning, you undertake tasks and invest your energy in activities that bring you true contentment because they nourish your heart and mind.

CHALLENGES FOR YOU

Use your intuition to choose one of these tools or invent one of your own:

- ♥ Develop and listen to your inner feelings to try to decode situations and people.
- ♥ Develop and use your extrasensory abilities such as clairaudience, clairvoyance or clear feeling.
- ♥ Abandon what is meaningless to you and commit to what is meaningful.

THE GODDESS

Key words: unity, alliance, healing,
potential, realisation, recognition

This card embodies the sacred feminine in all its splendour and light. The Goddess possesses all seven archetypal energies present in this oracle:

- ♥ the Amazon
- ♥ the Matriarch
- ♥ the Child-woman
- ♥ the Maternal Woman

- ♥ the Sensual Woman
- ♥ the Accomplished Woman
- ♥ the Mystic Woman.

The Goddess knows her resources, qualities and strengths. She taps into them to realise her potential, flourish and find fulfilment in life. She expresses these resources, qualities and strengths fearlessly and unashamedly with rightness of the heart.

The Goddess is aware of her wounds, taking care to treat them so they don't become obstacles. Her aim is to continue to grow and elevate herself. Each day the Goddess frees herself further from past memories to connect with her original essence and embody her true nature found in her innermost being.

The Goddess has healthy, balanced, nourishing and fulfilling friendships as well as work, love and sexual relationships, in which she can always be herself.

The Goddess is aware of her shadows; she observes them benevolently and from a distance to free herself from them and head towards greater light.

The Goddess's chakras are open and regulated so she can shine and express the different dimensions of her being.

Finally, the Goddess has deep self-knowledge; she knows who she truly is and she lives authentically and uniquely. She is connected to her true essence, so she may express herself fully.

INVITATION

This card invites you to:

- ♥ Become aware of your qualities, strengths and resources.
- ♥ Treat your wounds.
- ♥ Bring harmony into your relationships.
- ♥ Transform your shadows.
- ♥ Open and regulate your chakras.
- ♥ Recognise yourself in all your splendour and deep essence, expressing yourself freely in your words and actions.
- ♥ Be authentic.

EXERCISE

This visualisation is to bring your inner Goddess to life.

STEP 1. Imagine the different goddesses you feel within you, letting them arise in your mind. You can draw them or symbols of them without trying to create anything pretty. Then, give them names that might translate their energies and determine which adjectives may describe them and their qualities and strengths.

STEP 2. Take your time to feel these goddesses. When they are fully present within you, feel yourself as a Goddess containing all these other goddesses. Imagine the resonance emanating from her, her power and light then confidently scatter this energy.

STEP 3. Repeat the following sentence, completing the missing words with what you feel or comes to your mind without limiting yourself: 'I am …'

STEP 4. Visualise yourself grounding these words, these energies, into the earth and the space around you. Your entire being shines with these energies.

STEP 5. Imagine you are a Goddess, then store that image and what it exudes inside you so you may revive it whenever you feel the need or call. To remember your inner Goddess, forge a durable link with her, connect with her easily and consciously and revive her presence and beneficial energies. You can also draw yourself as a Goddess: visualise a symbol that reminds you of her, like an energetic tattoo, or find or create a piece of jewellery to wear.

ABOUT THE
AUTHOR

Malory Malmasson is a therapist gifted with subtle perceptions. She dedicates much of her life to spreading spirituality-centred messages of love and consciousness. Through her works she tries to bring her insights and guidance to a new generation, with advice and practical tools grounded in her time.

www.femininsacre.fr

ABOUT THE ILLUSTRATOR

Marion Blanc is an illustrator and graphic designer. With her illustrations she creates a dream world in which she softly represents nature and femininity, among other subjects. Marion looks to communicate emotions and bring a touch of sensitivity through her work. Colour choices are of paramount importance in her creations.

www.behance.net/marionblanc